Life During School

Prince Yaduvanshi

About The Author

Hi friends, I am Prince from Mumbai, India. Currently I am a class 11 science student at Mithibai College, Mumbai. I love reading books. I write books on my personal experience.

Social Handles:-

Linkedin - **Prince Yaduvanshi**
Instagram - **princeyaduvanshi015**

How to read this book

As there is no conventional method to read books. Some like to read it by holding, some read by putting fingers or pen on words,etc.But for the best output, following are some good tips to read it efficiently,

1. First just go through the book as we do with cards.

2. Read the index so that you can get the headings and then read according to it.

3. Use your finger or a pointer to read, so that you can't get distracted from outside.
4. Try creating a picture/imagine the situation written in the book.

Contents

Introduction

Education is one of those basic needs which is required to each and every individual, citizen of the nation. Nations growth is directly proportional to the percentage of people educated. Education helps us in understanding things, helps to challenge things, and is beneficial for making the right decision in a dilemma.Also people with good education background get opportunities of getting high profile jobs and they reach superior positions.

Earlier during the ancient period, there was a gurukul education system. In which saints, disciples used to teach life lessons from vedic literatures, ancient books, vedas, learnings from various warriors, meditation, biographies, etc. In those periods people used to travel in different towns, cities, nations, etc. The classes used to be held in temples. Over the period various subjects for example philosophy, psychology, math, physics,etc were included.

Unfortunately, in 1835, the Gurukul education system disappeared and the modern system of English Education was brought to India by Lord Macaulay. By this change schools were made and a new education system was started in India and this education system is still in race. As education is one of the basic needs which substitute human intelligence and memory, a child is admitted in a school right from the age 3-5 in India.

This book is all about my journey as a school student from the genesis of my first school in village to class 10th termination. You will discover a glimpse of some short stories, for example My childhood school, incidents occurring, friends who left us, my haunting speech on farewell day, what I learned from school, online lectures & online exams, some failure stories, more about friends, teachers, etc.

I assured you that all the readers will relate it with themselves and their past in the school and will learn so many things. It will take you towards the journey of your childhood. Now just try to remember some memorable moments when you used to be in school.

In the initial portion of this book you will find some early school stories and you'll get to know more about me and ahead there are some more interesting incidents. Also, this book ends up with a small message for all of the readers, so don't forget to read that last chapter once you finish reading 30 chapters.

CHAPTER 1

Going School for first Time

In 2011 when I was ready to go to school my one of the uncles who used to live with us in the village bought a bag for me, it was blue in color. Next day I was admitted to a nearby school in Azamgarh, Uttar Pradesh. It was inside the main Market of Jainagar. There were 10+ classrooms with no benches in Sr.kg class but right from class 1-8 there were benches in all the classes. So we used to sit on a yellow mat. At that time I was a 4-5 year old boy.

One of my cousin's brother Vishal also took admission in that same school after some days. He was 5 years old and we both used to come to school with sons of my fathers friend. They all were elders and were studying in higher classes than us. Every morning at 7 o'clock we used to go to their home and then when they got ready we marched towards our school which was 1 km far from our village Basupur.It was a Hindi medium school, the teacher used to teach us Hindi vowels, consonants. They were telling us to make zero 50 times everyday and other numbers and so on.

Sometimes we both the cousin brothers, me and Vishal used to bath, swim in the canals passing through our village. Sometimes I used to come with my grandfather to wash cows, buffaloes while grazing them in the farms. We used to jump in the flowing water of canals from the pools. I remember once I was contacted with an earth worm and then I was a little scared then my grandfather removed it with the help of his stick.

The people of all the villages contributed to organize the Mela. It was near my school. There is a huge crowd surrounding the mela. You will find each and everything in the shops, you can watch lots of dramas, and you can find almost each and every famous Indian Sweet(Mithai).

Short story

One day my mother put a roti roll with papers in the bottle space of the bag and tiffin in the lower chain. During recess, I didn't find a roti in the whole bag, I thought she forgot to put it. I told Vishal this to my cousin brother Vishal, and he ran away home to bring it but did not return back after the recess. In those days, I have heard stories of a Saint(Jogi) in saffron clothes who kidnaps children and takes them away. I thought my cousin brother Vishal was taken away by such a Saint. That is why he has not returned till now.I was too anxious and nervous.

In the evening when I went back home with my neighbors, I found absolute silence in my house, I was worrying about what would I say if my family members ask me where Vishal is?. After some time they asked me where Vishal was. I was shocked, really Vishal didn't come here? I told he is coming with Sunny and his brother. Afterwards Vishal came with my grandfather, he had gone with him to help my grandfather in the fields. Now I am satisfied and fine seeing Vishal in front of me.

Then at night my mother showed where she had kept the chapatis. Also all the family members told me not to come alone, otherwise jogi will catch us and take us with him. They all were annoyed. I studied for almost 2 months in that school and then I went to live at my Nani's house with my mother and continued my studies from there. Read the next chapter for getting more about it.

CHAPTER 2

My First school

In 2011, when I was shifted to Nani's village near Varanasi,Uttar Pradesh I was living with my mummy, nani, aunty. There was only one school which was near , so at that time I was admitted to a lower division class called 'A'. The school was very small. It has only three small classrooms, with divisions 'A','B','C'. There were no standards like 1,2..10. There were no benches we used to sit on the floor.

Every morning my mother used to wake me and my sister.She bathed us and made us wear yarn sweaters, which was tailored by my mother. We get ready and she holds my sister's hands from one side and my hand from another side. We have to walk for 15 minutes through the middle of the fields to reach the school.

While walking I used to see the whole fields, I used to see farmers of our and nearby villages working in them,waters flowing in the fields through the canals or tubules, huge mango and banyan trees making noise whenever there was a flow of wind.Green fields with grains, sugarcanes, sunflower, pora(. shepherd with sheeps, goats, cowherd with cows.

My Nani, mother, and aunties say that I was very cute in my childhood so everyone used to love me and whenever people see me in the way they used to smile and give me something to eat. For example :- toffee, gud, etc.

It is very common in Uttar Pradesh, during suitable seasons due to flow of wind the fruits like mangoes,jamun fall down. So while going with my mummy towards school, I used to run leaving my mothers hands to see whether mangoes had fallen or not.When I got those mangoes or jamun I used to keep them in my bag and eat them when I got back home. As My school was on the other side of the road, my mother helped us to cross the road and left me and my sister in the school.

I don't know why? But When I used to see my mother going back home through the green fields I became emotional. At that moment I used to think that I'll never go home now, the teachers will catch me. Sometimes my mother turned to see me while walking, I used to say bye-bye moving my tiny hands even she.

The teacher's only taught us the alphabet, numbers from 1-100 in 'A'. I was willing to go in division 'B'. But for that I'll have to wait for 1 year. After 1 year My father brought me and my mother to Mumbai. My school days and experience,friends in Mumbai school will be covered in detail ahead.

Dear Friends, Now whenever i visit my grandmother's village during vacations. I visit my previous school. I feel very sad to say that now that school has become abandoned. Still I can see the blackboards with chalk dust, broken chairs, written names on walls, etc. I sat on the floor and feeled the 10 year old vibe.

There was a small temple near the school. Where I used to pray during my exams and sit whenever I used to feel low. I loved that place a lot, because the whole place was very silent,peacefull and I used to throw stones in the small canals full of water flowing beside that temple .Dear readers, I miss those days a lot living among the beautiful natural places in the village, there was no tension,stress.

CHAPTER 3

My one month in Mumbai school

It was 2012, June when me and my mother came to the city of dreams, Mumbai. After one or two weeks my father took me and we went to Swami Vivekananda High School,Jogeshwari to get admission into it.

As it is a very long process to get admission in Mumbai schools. First you'll need to submit important documents and then you are admitted. So after getting admission, my mother came to leave me in school, as parents were not allowed inside the school during study hours the watchmen or peon took me to a classroom.

It was a completely new world for me because I was a villager who used to sit on the mat in my school in my village .Literally I was getting anything, what the teacher was saying or teaching. I was sitting in that classroom for almost one month. As on the last day of the month the teacher collected the whole students calendar for writing the no.of present days and absent days of the students. So that parents should know that his/her child is active in school.

Before going ahead, let me tell you something weird. In that 1 month, I have never raised my hands to say," present" for attendance because I did not know how to talk in hindi. Also, I was not aware of the roll number system. As I was very new to such things, I have never tried to ask the teacher.

I was sitting on the third bench and the teacher called my name,'Prince, what is your standard'? I was thinking about what she is asking. As I was silent, she asked in Hindi. I was still silent '. She checked in the calendar that I am in Sr.kg. But still by mistake I was sitting in Third standard from last 1 month.

She took me to Sr.kg class and told me that this is your real class,you should sit here from tomorrow onwards. At that time I was very nervous facing that incident but today I am very glad to have that story to share with you all.After this day I started sitting in Sr.kg class and learnt a little bit of Hindi by listening and talking to some of my friends. Now at this point I can speak 4 languages.

CHAPTER 4

Prize not obtain

In Senior kg I was very lucky to get the role of Ganesha during the annual day function. I was selected for that role because of my audition taken by the teachers. I had devoted 1 month to practicing dance with my dance teacher in school. I was exhilarated to be a part of that function.

On the day of the occasion I came to school with my mother, she was sitting in the audience and I was standing backstage with my fellow classmates, preparing for the presentation. I was in the Ganesha Mask and had clothes identical to him. We danced to the Jai Ganesh song . I'll share the picture if I find it.

After the performance, we thought that now the entire program had ended and then I told my mother to go home. Next day the teacher told me that we were calling your name yesterday for the prize distribution where you were? I told that we went home. At that time I was thinking I should have stopped there the previous day so I would have received a certificate along with some gifts. But time had passed away and I was left with regret.

CHAPTER 5

My interest in studies & sports

Studies

I was on the black list of failed students till class 3rd. I was so damn that I used to mark the 2nd question's answer from the option given in the 1st question and repeated this whole process for the rest of the questions.

I used to get marks like 5/30, 7/30,etc.Due to which no one used to talk with me. Teachers used to shout at me. But when I came in 4th standard I started observing the students who had scored well. I followed them. In 3rd and previous classes the teachers should think while correcting whether they should pass me or not.

But after observing the topper of my class, I learned something which gave me results when I followed them. Now the teacher should think while correcting whether she should give 30/30 or 29/30. Yes, she deducts one mark in languages but gives full marks in other subjects like math, science,etc.

Now when I see my previous class papers I used to laugh at the way I used to solve papers and on my previous marks. From 5th standard there was a ranking system, whoever scored high marks in the whole class the teacher should take his/her name.

I remembered that in the first unit test of class 5th, Adarsh was first with 94/95 marks, Aakash on second, Aayush on third, Samir on 5th and I was in 4th position with 91/95. It is true that I always secured 1,2, or 3 rank in every class exam. From sixth to Tenth standard.

Sports

When I was in the primary section from class 1-4. There used to be sports events held in the month of October or November every year in Vaastu ground,Jogeshwari by our school for the primary students. I have participated in many games like Sack race, wearing the sweater, running race, passing the ball,etc.

This scenario is different because I haven't won any games. From class 5th-10th we were having 2 extra outdoor games like kabaddi and cricket. As I was good in both the games I was in, playing 11 in cricket and starting 7 in kabaddi , our team was very strong in both games so we won the trophy for our class in both the games. There was a time when I was believing that I will be a cricketer in my future like others. But now I realize that it was just an illusion in which I was surviving.

Note:- **If you haven't decided your goal, purpose of your life then do read the book 'Ikigai'. It will help you to understand yourself better and find your passion.**

But right from class 6th I stopped taking part in other games like running races of different ranges, relay race, passing the ball, frog jump, sack race,etc. Excluding cricket & kabaddi because I used to think that If i'll participate no matter how well I execute I'll lose. So it is better to stay at home and study for exams.

But, now I think that I should have gone there and participated in those games and competed with my fellow friends, and I would have learned a lot through it. So, please avoid these mistakes. Now also on each and every sunday, I gather my friends, my elders and we gio to play cricket on the roads. But that doesn't mean I'll become a cricketer.

CHAPTER 6

Praying to god for happening good

"God is most glorified in us when we are most satisfied in Him." "God loves each of us as if there were only one of us." "God never said that the journey would be easy, but He did say that the arrival would be worthwhile." Earlier when I was 8-9 years I used to question people whether god really exists. Is there any spiritual power running this world peacefully?

As the time passed away I got to know about it and experienced such spiritual powers. One of my Spiritual Guru Tribhuvan Nath Sharma told us that when you believe in god, then god exists but if you don't believe in his existence then he is probably not present. So just believe and you will probably feel and receive its benefit.

In smaller standards like 6th, 7th, 8th standard I used to say 'Jai Hanuman' many times in my mind whenever there was an extremely harsh situation, problematic situation. This would have helped me to secure myself from troubles. One such example is, If the teacher is showing any paper then at those times I used to chant 'Jai Hanuman, Jia Hanuman' consistently until I received my own paper in my hand. Believe me, 95 out of a hundred times I have seen whatever marks I was expecting. Yes before seeing that day you need to do your karma, hard work.

In class 10th January prelims my all the papers were very well but geography was one of the papers which was not as good as I was thinking. I was expecting 32-33. Because in the geography paper I had made a lot of mistakes.(Geography paper was not shown till now) One day our geography subject teacher came for lectures. Everyone was asking whether she had corrected all the papers or not, then she replied,"She is not finished with checking, geography paper will be shown on some other day". She told me that other students in my class have scored out in geography. I was shocked to hear that because I was going to score very less marks in it.

Today, the teacher will show us a geography paper and While going to school in the morning I was continuously chanting 'Jai Hanuman' throughout the whole trip. 30-40% students have scored 38-39. When the teacher was bound to give my paper I thought she would shout at me when she saw that I had scored only 30-33 marks. But dear readers I was shocked when I saw 40/40 marks in my paper. It was like magic for me. Just imagine if you have taken any lottery ticket and when you match your number the shopkeeper says you have owned 10 and hearing that you become sad and suddenly he says 10 crores. The experience was like that.

My dear readers, I am sure you might be praying to god in your hardships if not then next time when you will have trouble pray to god in that circumstance and just see what happens.

CHAPTER 7

Day in the life as a school student

Have you ever seen a day in the life videos on youtube or on other social media platforms. For example day in the life as an IIT-Jee aspirant, day in the life of an entrepreneur, Day in the life of a Neet aspirant, etc. But have you ever seen a day in the life of a school student? If not then you will get to know in this chapter.

Our school was a combination of both hindi & english medium. The classes for Hindi medium students should run from 1 PM to 6 PM and for English medium students right from the morning 7:05-12:30.

I used to wake up at 6 AM in the morning and get ready, and then I used to have tea-rotti or sometimes fried rice made by my mother. After that I used to walk for 20-25 minutes to reach my school. I have hardly taken a rickshaw during my school life, I love to walk as it is good for physical health.

As I was living in andheri(east) and my school was in jogeshwari(east) the distance is around 2-2.5 km from my house andI would have become tired while returning.

Sometimes I used to meet students who are my friends. We used to talk about the latest news, for example on cricket, kabaddi,etc. And mostly on studies and upcoming exams. I don't know whether you people have noticed or not that when we are traveling with others or going together we don't realize the flow of time. We feel that how early we reached the destination.

I used to reach on time everyday at my school. But sometimes it becomes 2-3 minutes late. So we have to stand on the ground floor of our school. Once the prayer ends the teacher or principal present their will sign on the calendar and then we get permission to enter in our classes.

When you reach on time, go to your class and stand for prayer and then once the prayer ends wish the teacher. And from this our daily classes used to start. The first class was always taken by the class teacher and rest by other subject teachers(From class 5th).

The recess or break used to be held from 10 AM to 10:30. The teacher goes away to have lunch and we the students start having whatever we used to bring. We also share it with each other.

Some of the friends who live near the school used to go home and have lunch. Also, we can buy samosa, pav bhaji, chinese foods,etc. During recess from outside our school. Sometimes I also have those 5 Rs samosa and 5 Rs pav bhaji. But generally I used to bring my tiffin.

Once the recess ends the rest of the subject classes run till 12:30.
Ideally speaking we feel energetic till 12 AM and then till the last period everyone starts feeling sleepy and boring. It depends on teacher to teacher whether they give you work, teach or they tell you to head down and rest.

At 12:25 there used to be a small prayer and then we left our school. We can see a massive crowd of students on the road walking, running, waiting for the bus, taking rickshaws and returning home. As there were two more schools near our school the crowd tripled. Also some parents wait outside for their child.

I always find some of my friends to go home together, the reason behind this has been revealed before. Normally I used to go with Ojas or Aditya. As Ojas was residing near my house and Aditya was in the middle way.

I used to return home at 1 AM. After that I used to rest and have some food till 1:30 AM. And then I start studying or doing my tuition/classes homework or when there is no work or less homeworks than I used to go for playing cricket with my friend Sumit.

I used to go for home tuition from 1st-9th from 4-6. Then after returning from my tuition or classes I was doing my school homeworks or studying or practicing math till 9:45 and then I used to have dinner in 10-15 minutes.Then I used to go for a walk near my house on the roads with my friends or with persons to whom I know. Also there was a silent and secret place where I was sitting, the description about this place will be given in the next chapter.

After this I used to sleep at 11 PM and repeat this whole schedule from Monday-friday. As there were holidays on saturday and sunday. I used to play cricket with my friends on these two days, do my homeworks, and go to tuition.

Situation got changed when I came in 9th standard

After coming back to Mumbai from my village after covid at the end of class 9th I used to get a lot of time to do extra things as our school lectures were online. I was ready to develop myself, my personality, etc. Now I started reading self-help books. I used to do meditation, running,etc. Whenever there is a holiday. This habit has made some positive changes in my life.

Mostly on Sunday and Saturday we used to play cricket matches between our same class and with different divisions A,B,C. At BMC ground Andheri or Vastu ground,Jogeshwari. Sometimes I really get stuck and feel low and sad that now those awesome days are never going to come again.

INFLUENCE
80/20
DRiVE
CREATIVITY, INC.
Who Moved My Cheese?
GETTING TO YES
TRIBE OF MENTORS
THE SUBTLE ART OF NOT GIVING A F*CK
5 SECOND RULE
EXTREME OWNERSHIP
THE HARD THING ABOUT HARD THINGS
DECISIVE
How to Measure Anything
What Got You Here Won't Get You There
GETTING EVERYTHING YOU CAN OUT OF ALL YOU'VE GOT
JAY ABRAHAM
DEEP WORK
FINISH
JON ACUFF
AWAKEN THE GIANT WITHIN
ROBBINS
THE GIFT OF FEAR
Playing Big
THE MILLIONAIRE NEXT DOOR
Bogleheads
THE 10X RULE
HAPPINESS
Sapiens
A Brief History of Humankind

CHAPTER 8

My third name in the school

I have come a long way now. 5 years have passed and I have been cured up from a type of chronic cough disease. I was diagnosed with it right from my childhood.When I was a 1-2 year old fellow I was diagnosed with pneumonia but it was cured.

I am sure you all have gone through a normal cold(Sardi) and how unpleasant, atrocious you feel in such sickness. The taste of things disappears, and the smelling power becomes very weak. But in case of chronic cough disease, you fall sick, cold for eight to ten weeks.

But in my case it was there for the whole year. I was experiencing that pain every single day. It is horrible for you and I wish no one should suffer from such a kind of disease. I had to keep a handkerchief whenever I go outside for school or tuitions so that I can wipe my nose continuously. Sometimes I was also not able to inhale and exhale properly, sometimes I used to respirate like a dog.

I was always scared of what people, my friends will think or say whenever I'll wipe my nose among them continuously. I used to sit on the last or second last bench, so that no one should communicate with me, I shouldn't come in the eyes of teachers. But still some of my friends knew and they used to call me by a funny name that I didn't like. Over the time every single student in my class used to call me with that name in class 2-4 th standard. Due to that I prefer not to say anything but from inside I used to feel low. Such things have made me an introverted guy and think when I am going to win this battle and become more sociable.

Once I remember in class 4th there was a cricket tournament organized by our school at Shivai ground, Jogeshwari. I was very keen to participate and play for my class. But students of our class made fun of me and declined me to join their team. They questioned my stamina, my disease. Such incidents had made me a very introverted, shy person. I was facing two challenges one was the disease I was suffering and second the fear of interacting with society i.e social problems.

My parents have taken me to a lot of doctors and done a lot of treatments to cure it, but still no one knows the root cause of it. Some doctors said I am suffering from pertussis, a lung infection . Thanks to my Biradar uncle who recommended Dr. Anand Pawar who did his treatment and cured me in just six months. Now I can really breathe deeper and I can inhale and exhale properly. Over the period the effect of cough got lesser and I finally got victory on it.

Now whenever I meet my school friends they say that earlier you were called by a name and now you are looking fine, that disease has cured. One of my far friends Anand used to call me by that funny name every time and has made me feel low among the whole class and also in front of some teachers. Now they feel sorry for insulting me, criticizing me when we were in school. I say,"It's okay, that was childish".

I'll request you all to not criticize, make fun, judge capabilities of others. We should always treat one another equally. Because we don't know how they are feeling? What is happening in their life? Are they happy or sad? So it's better to be treated normally as we do with others.

CHAPTER 9

My friends in school

You all have heard or read the quote,'Your life is directly reflected by your peer group and friends with whom you live'. All the students studying in the class were my friends but there were some of the friends with whom I love to stay and share each other's opinions, share notes, talk about exams.

I remember my first friends were nagesh, saumya and shubham in senior Kg. Saaumya and Shubham both studied till high school but on the other hand Nagesh left the school after Senior Kg. And after that we didn't meet. I am sure he has forgotten me and we can never meet again.

You all know that when you are continuous in the class lectures in the same school, so within some period the whole class knows you and you know other students.

But I have read somewhere that we shouldn't make friends with everyone. I was having good friendship with some of my friends like Shivam Yadav, Shivam Rai, Samir Khan, Adarsh Singh, Adarsh Yadav, Gaurav Yadav, Sahil Ansari, Hardik Soni,

Kundan Yadav, Nilesh Yadav, Arpit Yadav, Aditya Pal, Divyansh Singh, Prince Kanojia, Aakash Maurya, Aayush Dubey, Vishnat Maurya, Aniket pandit and others.

They all were good in their own field. For example both the shivam were good in cricket and athletics. They were awarded with best sportsperson of the year in our schools many times. Samir, Adarsh Singh were good at kabaddi. Adarsh, Aayush and Aaksh were toppers of our school.

Vishant Maurya is one of the best cricket players from our school. He has got man of the match many times for his astounding performance in cricket tournaments. Apart from sports, all my friends were very serious about their studies.

I have learnt a lot through them, for example simplicity, team spirit by playing with them, humbleness, curiosity, integrity,etc. Also I have never seen anyone fighting or abusing each other. Maybe I haven't observed but they have respect for me and I was respectful for them.

CHAPTER 10

Free fire trauma and exams.

In this age of globalization, digitalisation it has become faster and easier to get anything in just a second. Nowadays people prefer not to go out and play outdoor games, indoor games they are playing video games, mobile games from their comfort zone at their home. The impact of video games are so bad that if you just download and play it once, your mind will say to play it once again and again you will get stuck in it addicted to it.

I have been the prey of this effect. In class 7th all of my friends used to play a game called 'free fire'. Before that we used to play cricket on grounds, but when this killer game entered their life they have forgotten everything. I have seen people shouting at other players, and heard firing sounds while playing this addictive game.

During Diwali vacation I used to be free for the whole day. I tried to convince my friends to play outside, but they were happy playing 'free fire' and Pubg.
Now I was helpless, so I decided to install and play Free Fire. I installed it and played the first game, I performed well so I played it many times. I was getting self gratitude when I used to kill opposite players. Every morning I used to wake up early not for studying only for playing that killer game.

I used to play it for 9-10 hours everyday. My friend Sumit used to come to my home, he used to support me whenever I played the game. He used to say,"Kill that one, pick this gun, go there" such things. I had planned that I'll close by playing it once the Diwali vacation ends. But still after coming from school I used to play it for 2-3 hours and then 4-5 hours at night till 12 clock. Due to which my eyes were paining, my sleep pattern was not good, and I felt tired in the morning.

I remember that when there were my exams, I used to play it instead of bothering about exams. Yes I was addicted to that game very badly. Somehow I wanted to get out of it, but still I was not able to do that. I used to give excuses to myself when I thought of deleting it. I had deleted it many times but whenever I see someone playing that game I used to download it again. But one day I decided to delete it forever, it was my inner voice who helped me to do it. Now four years have passed and I have never installed it again. Yeah! Sometimes I play it when I see some of my friends play in their free time, just for entertainment. If you are in the same situation as I was previously, please delete it otherwise it may affect your health, sleeping pattern, will make you more exhausted in normal conditions, you may face some mental health problems.

Instead play games like chess which require a lot of effort to play and it will help you to build your logical and critical thinking skills better. Instead play outdoor games like cricket, kabaddi, football, do some physical exercise. This will help you to grow more.

CHAPTER 11

The chess Manifesto

Once I was watching a movie with my friend Sumit and heard that if you play chess, you become more intelligent, genius, etc. So we decided to purchase chess. We went to the Supreme store, Deepak store to get it but it was very expensive so while returning we bought it for very cheap ₹20 from a mini shop. We were happy, but didn't know how to play. So we started observing elders who used to play it on a daily basis and learned how many steps each and every character moves.

Me and Sumit started playing it and over the period we learned to play very well. I started playing with some elders and used to lose every time I played.
The day came when I was able to have victory over them and gained some confidence. I learned some shortcut hacks or tricks to checkmate anyone in just 3-4 moves.

I got an opportunity to participate in a school chess contest when I was in class 8. I was having 1 week to practice with my friend Sumit. Every morning I wake up, I used to think that I had won the chess contest and received a certificate from the Principal every single day. Yes it was fantasy. The day came and I was called into the playing room. I signed and was waiting for my opponent to come. Then one guy came. I don't recognize his name, but he was playing very well. He was from class 8th B.He gave me a lot of checks and each time I should think that now I am gone. Our game runned for approximately half an hour but in the end I defeated him.

Next to him I played 2-3 more games with other students who were from either class 8th or class 7th and defeated them as well. No, I was called to play a final match on Saturday. I was keen to know who is that person with whom I have to play the final match. Somehow I got to know one of my friends told me that now you won't be able to have a victory and win the tournament. I was really stunned hearing the words of my friends.

I went to play the final match but coincidentally my opponent didn't come. He was absent.According to rules & regulation I have won the final match. So Sandesh Sir made me the winner. I was very glad with my achievement. I entered my class, my friends were waiting and believing that I had lost the final match, but when I narrated the incident of winning the chess tournament they all became horrified and congratulated me. Though I was happy but still I was musing that it would have been a great feeling if I had really defeated Sanket.

Dear readers this was not the end of this story. Next day Sir came with Sanket who was my opponent with whom I had to play yesterday, as he was absent I was made winner. Sir asked,"Are you ready to play with him"? For a few seconds I entered the world of conundrum. I know that Sanket is a very good player and I can lose. But still I said,"Yes". Let me tell you an incident when I was in class 2nd, me and Sanket where classmates and sitting together our class teacher told us to slap each other, because we were not paying attention Sanket slapped me and then I slapped him with my full potential. After getting that slap his facial expressions were showing that he was crying from inside. I felt sorry for that thing.

There was utter silence in the playing room. There was a table with a chess setup upon it, two chairs for Prince(me) and my opponent Sanket.For a couple of seconds I thought that I have come a long way defeating 4-5 peoples and I can win too. We started playing, and in just 2-3 minutes I defeated Sanket. On this day I really feel that there are some powers in the universe through which you really achieve anything. Reason behind this is because before the tournament I was continuously practicing chess with my friend and believing that I have won the chess tournament. In the end, the same thing happened to me.

CHAPTER 12

School student during rainy season

In my early years of school during rainy seasons, I used to wear raincoats as small childrens do. The whole body gets packed excluding the area below our knee, so that only parts get wet below your knee. As the rainy season started I used to go to the raincoat shop with my mother and she used to choose the most designed one every time. Those raincoats which had cartoon characters drawing i.e. doraemon, tom and Jerry, Chhota bheem but most of the raincoats had mickey mouse printed on it.Hardly, I have chosen any designed raincoat because I don't like such things, even now in the present circumstance I wear those tshirts or shirts which doesn't have too much designs printed on it.

As I became older I started using umbrellas for protecting myself from water as all the people use. From class 5th to 10th we were having huge paints as a school uniform. In umbrella the lower part used to get wet but within half an hour it got dry. I remember it was Sunday and we were playing cricket on the roads and suddenly it started raining and still we played cricket. One of my friends named it rain cricket. It was a wonderful experience playing cricket in the rain.

Some regions of Mumbai in the rainy season. Due to high consistent rainfall it used to be filled with water. The level of water on the roads reached upto our knees sometimes. Such areas include the playgrounds, roads and the railway station. The situation of roads near my school had become like that so we cross it carefully. While crossing some students threw water on others and made them annoyed.

When I was in class 6th, while crossing the road in such a water I slipped down and my books from the bag got wet. Some of the students were laughing in that situation, some of them helped me to get out of that marsh. Everyone was staring at me, I sat on the footpath and was thinking how I should go inside the school in such an atrocious condition. I was very sad, because my books got wet and there was an exam nearby. I was thinking about how I will study? It was an extremely bad situation for me on that day. Thanks to my class teacher and my dear friends who helped me to complete my book.

When we believe that there is less probability of getting rain today and we go to school without an umbrella, if the rain starts in the middle I used to find some place where I can stand for a couple of minutes and move towards school when the intensity of rain becomes less. In most of the situations I was left out with less time so I used to find students who are my and have an umbrella so that they can share it with and we can reach our destination together i.e. our school.

If I was lucky, I'll get my friends in the mid-journey and they share an umbrella with me and while talking we reached school. Have you ever experienced or did such things?

CHAPTER 13

Lockdown period and online school

During the lockdown period our studies went online with the help of gadgets, apps, websites for example zoom, google meet, microsoft offices,etc. In the initial phase of online classes our school staff has made a whatsapp group for particular classes. They used to send recorded videos on chapters. But over time they started conducting our live classes on zoom.

At that time I was in my village and I used to enjoy it a lot there. I hardly joined any class. I thought, instead of joining these boring online lectures, let's learn from youtube. I have wasted lots of time in finding which video is best and good for watching to understand any particular concept. Apart from this I was also not studying from an exam perspective. This means I was not memorizing the definitions, formulas, only things I used to understand the concept and just going through how it works in real life.

I was watching a podcast on Ranveer Allahabdia's channel and suddenly I got a message on whatsapp highlighting we have online exams after one week. I was under pressure reading that note. I somehow managed to study and covered 75%

of the portion and gave each and every paper excluding geography. Reason behind this is that in villages you only get 10-15 hours of electricity and there will be a lot of cutouts between them, so at night I forgot to plug my phone in for charging. It was the winter season and there was fog in the surrounding area and you won't be able to guess the time. My paper was from 8 am and I woke up at 8:35 am. Yes, the exam was over.

At the end of class 9th online semester exam the teacher had given some assignments to complete and submit in the school on a suitable date. But my situation was different, I was in my native place at that time and I didn't prefered to complete assignments, I took that lightly. Due to that I lost some percent. Over this whole exam period I have never tried to copy or paste from google or find answers from the book as some of the students used to do once a teacher from our school said. Because" The most important thing in the world is trust, it can take years to build but seconds to lose".Overall I scored 75-80 % in my class 9th.

CHAPTER 14

Village coaching in lockdown

During the time of lockdown all the companies, startups, factories, cinema hall, railway stations, airplanes, etc were closed. After living in suffocation for almost 3 months in Mumbai during lockdown we went to our village near Varanasi, Uttar Pradesh. My school was online on zoom.

I remember it was the month of December and the temperature was very low. In the environment it was the winter season. We all have to wear sweaters throughout the whole day. The water was colder than water from the refrigerator. I was studying with the help of youtube from youtube channels like Pawan Wagh academy, dinesh sir, jr tutorials, etc.

It's very common in the Yadav family that all the Yaduvanshi keep cows and buffaloes in their houses. Some of them usually depend on the milk products which they will make and sell in the market to make a profit and for living. There were some cows and buffaloes in our village. Every morning my grandfather woke up and after milking he used to distribute that milk through his biki(scooter like vehicle) to one of the teachers residing inside the Gram Samaj P.G college Jainagar.

My grandfather asked me if I want to study so I can take help from that teacher. At midnight he called the teacher and I talked with him. The conclusion was that I was an English medium student. He can't teach an English medium student. After that my grandfather connected to some well known people from our village who really know some capable teachers to teach his grandson Prince Yaduvanshi.

Someone suggested a well-known teacher who runs his coaching in Jayanagar(Jigani) nearby. My grandfather said,"He is a very famous teacher, he has a lot of experience , he has taught your father, uncle, aunties). Now hearing this I was scared, I don't know the reason behind this. Next day I went with my grandfather. It was 11 o'clock in the morning and there was a group of cycles lying outside that coaching. There was a pitch dark path and in the end there was a classroom with some benches and some of the students of class 5th-6th were studying, I guess. I said, "Namaskar" to the teacher.

Then My grandpa introduced me to the teacher and told him that my grandson lives in Mumbai and studies there only, in lockdown they came here in a rural area. He requires a teacher who can teach him. I was very nervous at that point, all the students were staring at me. Sir asked me some questions which were very simple and I had given them very confidently. He told me to come in the evening at 4 o'clock.

In reality I don't want to go somewhere else and study. Instead I was happy and satisfied from watching youtube videos. As my grandpa was putting lots of effort for my betterment I was compromising. In the evening I went with a book, pen on a cycle. When I was parking my cycle, some students saw me and they were asking if I was Lavkush's nephew. I said yeah. When I entered the room the gossipings of students in Bhojpuri turned into silence. Some students were from my village.

Some of them greeted me and I sat near one of my village's students. Then after half an hour at 4:30 half an hour late the teacher came. I thought that now he would introduce myself with my fellow classmates. ButI was wrong . Sir took the attendance and then he asked some of the students why they were absent yesterday. I think everyone should know the answers given by 3-4 students. One student said,"I was absent because I had gone to find my aunt's son, my cousin who was lost". Hearing this legendary reason everyone laughed in a chuckling voice for a few minutes.One student said,"There was my uncle's engagement ceremony, I was busy in it". Sir said,"I think all the responsibility was on you?". The class started laughing.

One student said,"Yesterday there were many guests in my house ,tor handle them my mother said not to go to class". Still everyone was laughing. Now the legendary answer,"I forgot that I have to go coaching". Sir said, "You didn't forget to eat but forget to come". Then sir asked for homeworks and ordered to stand those who had not done their homeworks and hit them with a long wooden stick.

Dear reader, I was shocked to hear these kinds of reasons because in a city like Mumbai students have just two reasons: 1st they were having fever, they got late.

Then he started teaching 'waves' in hindi 'tarange'. First he dictated its definition in hindi. Then in the beginning he gave some good examples for example :- the mobile networks are in the form of waves, internet, etc. But when he asked some students to give such examples. The students gave many funny answers and the whole class used to laugh at it.

One of the students said that during the winter season when I go in the field near the lake the womens whispering about the conditions of their home, how her mother in law treats her can be heard very clearly due to the vibrations of the water in the form of waves. Hearing this everyone started laughing including the teacher. Sir said,"Yes, good example". Then one another student said that one day when I was going to my school on cycle the wind velocity was more and I heard the sounds of dog barking, hearing that I got scared and got back to home. Everyone was laughing at it.

Everyone sitting in the classroom belongs to hindi medium school, but I was the only guy from english medium school. Also, I was not able to get most of the points that sir was teaching. At 6 o'clock I went back home. My grandfather was watching the news on T.V. He asked me what I learnt, I said,"Many things, but it is hindi medium coaching". I was scared of going to that coaching the next day. So I decided not to go there. I continued my studies online through youtube channels.

It was a wonderful experience in studying village coachings, one of my cousin brothers who lives in the village told me that they get such kinds of enjoyment each and everyday.

CHAPTER 15

My coin collection Hobby

A **hobby** is considered to be a regular activity that is done for enjoyment, typically during one's leisure time. Hobbies include collecting themed items and objects, engaging in creative and artistic pursuits, playing sports, or pursuing other amusements. Participation in hobbies encourages acquiring substantial skills and knowledge in that area.

A list of hobbies changes with renewed interests and developing fashions, making it diverse and lengthy. Hobbies tend to follow trends in society, for example stamp collecting was popular during the nineteenth and twentieth centuries as postal systems were the main means of communication, while video games are more popular nowadays following technological advances. The advancing production and technology of the nineteenth century provided workers with more leisure time to engage in hobbies. Because of this, the efforts of people investing in hobbies has increased with time.

During the year 2015-2016 there was a huge amount of concrete gathered in our locality. I was playing with my friends and then I found a radish circular coin. I brought it and kept it in my house and then went to play once again and found 2-3 more coins. I was very glad to have those coins with me, I washed them and went to buy something to eat with the help of those coins. The shopkeeper didn't took those coins. I was sad, then an uncle who was involved in his small electronics business came and took those coins from me and gave 5 rupee coins in exchange of those rusted coins.

After some time, when I asked that uncle why he did that?Then he explained that these coins are from Saudi Arabia and they are quite old, that's why he took them from me. I attempted to get those coins back from him, but he refused to return them. After a month I found a small brown coin from somewhere. It was one cent from the United States of America, there was a picture of Abraham Lincoln on one side and of white house on the second side.. After that incident I kept asking people whether they have foreign coins or ancient indian coins. Most of them say,"No". I told many of my school friends but still I was not receiving any result from it.

One day, Akash Tiwari bought a 50 euros gold coloured coin to show me. I was keen to take that coin with me. I tried a lot to get it but he was not convinced to give it to me forever. Then in the recess he was very exhausted and feeling low, he wanted to eat samosa so he needed some money. I gave him money and he gave that coin to me to keep it forever. After some time almost everyone knew about my coin collection hobby including teachers.

I used to receive 3-4 coins every week from each one of my friends, mostly from muslim ones. Because their grandfather or grandmother goes to Dubai, Saudi, etc. for a tour. Till 10th standard I was so much involved in this thing that I have collected 100s of coins, some 5-8 notes. In lockdown period when I went to my Nan's village 70% of the coins that I have collected I put them in a small pot filled soil and digged it into the ground. Now I am left out with 30-40 coins with me. Also I have given some coins to villagers for friendship.

One day I met my friend's friend whose name is Govind. He was also a coin collector, he had many silver coins and some strange unrecognizable coins. When he got to know about my hobby he gifted me some strange unrecognizable coins, for example Elizabeth 1000 tokens. It was approximately 100 years old and very valuable. I called some professional coin collectors with the help of google and talked with them about selling those coins. He said,"He will give me 1500 for each coin". I refused to sell.

There was a small hole in that coin-like token. So one of my uncles requested me to give it to him, so that he can tie it in his hand or neck. I believed and gave him. When after one year I went to my village and asked him about that coin he said,"He has lost it". I was very sad. Also one of my tuition friends Bhavesh had given me an 1985s old 5 rupee coin on which there was a pic of Indira Gandhi. It was one of the most valuable coins of India. Seeing me doing coin collection influenced some of my friends to get them involved in this. They also started collecting coins. You all will be surprised to know that In my class 5th result my class teacher Kavita Mam wrote coin collector in hobbies as a remark.

Also, I had an Indian coin on which there is a picture of Indira Gandhi.Whose current value was approximately 4 lakh indian rupees. I have kept it in the pot with other coins and dug and put it inside the land in my village.

CHAPTER 16

Think Positive Get Positive

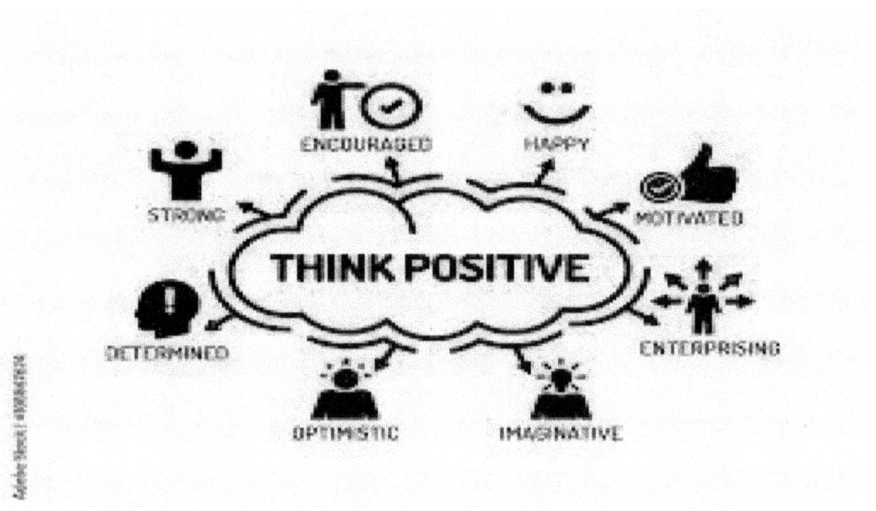

In class 10th in the month of january there was our class 10th prelims. Our science 1 teacher Mr.Praveen Dubey sir challenged us that one who will score 40/40 in his subject he will receive a gift and great applause in the class in simple words respect from him and others. He said,"Is there anyone in the class who can accept this challenge and really make it successful?' I accepted the challenge but not raised my hands to show that yes I am the only man who can do this. Even no one raised his/her hand.

I studied day and night for achieving doing that but on the day of science 1 exam, they canceled it and kept it in the last in the termination of the exam. I was well prepared and was confident that yes I can really obtain that maximum mark. When I saw the question paper, my heart sank, I was totally blind. The paper was beyond the expectation and also broke the rules of the board's paper pattern. There were more conceptual questions than theoretical questions.

I thought, if I feel that the paper is very difficult for me then it is difficult for other students as well. Through this motive I started solving papers and gave my best. Coming out of the school everyone was talking regarding the difficulty level of the paper. I was sure that I couldn't get 40/40. There were two reasons, first is that the paper was tricky and I have written all the answers in my own words and the second reason was that the teacher may check the paper strictly. I was knowing that now I am not in the game of getting 40/40 and couldn't receive an appreciation from sir.

When I came outside of the exam hall everyone was discussing the paper. Some of them say that he/she may have failed in this paper. It was confirmed that the paper was really tough. On the way I met some of my fellow friends checking the answers from the book. I went there because I don't want to discuss the answers because it lowers our self confidence and makes us feel inferior than others when you have done something wrong in the paper and get to know when you check the papers.

On Monday we were expecting that Science sir would show the paper to us, but excluding him all the teachers showed the paper. Sir promised that he will show us on Thursday because he is involved in checking the papers. Next day it was the second lecture and while entering he asked who Prince Yadav was. At that point I was very nervous and in a very low tone voice I raised my hand and said,"Me sir". Sir knows me very well but maybe he didn't know my name. He used to call me 'Yadavji'. He asked me from where you have written the answers in the science paper. I said the paper was tough and all the reasons, answer in one sentence I have written on my own.

Sir said to everyone in the class that I have told you all not to follow any guide, masterkey, navneet digest for writing answers in case of science. Also never try to learn the answers, instead understand the concept. I thought sir was saying to me, so I replied,"I didn't follow any guide or digest". Sir said,"I am not saying to you, I am talking to everyone. At that point I was too nervous and that lecture was terrible, all my friends were seeing me terribly, I was sad. Some of them were laughing seeing me in these bad circumstances. All of my friends were thinking that I have learnt all the answers and written them on paper because sir is shouting at me indirectly.

After sir's lecture got over everyone was staring at me, especially those who were going to fail in that paper. I took this situation negatively and was thinking that maybe I failed in this exam and that is why sir was talking regarding me or sir might be thinking that I have by heart all the answers and written in the paper. One of my friends, Arpit Yadav, told me to take whatever sir told you today. I was like “Haan”.

On Thursday sir came with the answer papers to show us. Before showing he clearly said that many of the students have failed and only few students have passed. Chanting has always helped me to move ahead from the problematic situations. I used to take God's name continuously in these circumstances. Sir started from roll no 1, roll no 2...roll no 9 failed. In girls there were only 2-3 of them who passed. A girl named ‘Ania’ in our class got 29-30/40. Sir said that I think that this is the highest mark from your class. After a long period our friends roll no came Arpit 31 or 32 Adarsh 33 and it was my roll no and sir repeated yes this is the highest marks from your class hearing that I was amazed I score 34/40. I was happy.

There was another student in our class whose name was Prince Gupta and he failed in science 1 so sir thought it’s me that is why he was asking yesterday. Sir checked my answer paper and said yes all the answers have been written by myself. I saw all of the students who were laughing at me a day before when sir asked me. They have failed and are scared and hiding behind bags or benches.

Believe me guys, your academic marks don't matter. No one is going to remember it and ask it to you even If you have failed. Your marks only matter in competitive examinations for selection. So just chill. One good thing about Amit Sir, Amit Classes Head, was that he had never forced us to obtain out off or good marks. The only thing he needed was that our concepts should be strong.

CHAPTER 17

Real Teachers Real Education

I believe that people who are successful today, who have achieved what they used to dream of because of their gurus, teachers. Also those who are trying hard but incapable of achieving their dreams and becoming successful in their life, then they should take guidance, help from their respective teachers,guide or mentor. Today we know Sachin Tendulakar because of his Coach Ramakant Achrekar. Swami Vivekanada because of the teachings and guidance of his guru Ramakrishna Paramahansa.

Every teacher has taught me something apart from academics. Our Science teacher Dubey Sir taught us never leave opportunities related to your field and your goal. He said,"It can be the key with which you can enter inside your goals bottom line" during one of his lectures. I learned the power of not reacting also how simply we can break a difficult problem and solve it easily from our mathematics teacher Sanjeev sir. I learned communication from our school headmaster. Simplicity from other teachers.

One teacher busted my myth, before I used to think that a person who speaks English fluently and uses difficult vocabulary in his conversation is good at communication. But she told me," Communication means how simple and easily you can share your thoughts among people".All the teachers used to explain the real life use of the concepts that they were going to teach us.

The priority of the guru, teacher is very crucial for our growth in our career. There is an doha by sant Kabirdas,"गुरू गोविन्द दोऊ खड़े, काके लागूं पांय।
बलिहारी गुरू अपने गोविन्द दियो बताय।।" This beautiful line explains that the teacher is mightier than god.

CHAPTER 18

School exams and friends marks

In our school there were four exams in each and every class right from 5th-10th. The first one was the first unit test which used to be held in August, First Semester before Diwali (An Indian Festival), Second unit test in January, Final Semester exams or Board exams for 10th standard students.

There was a ranking system in our school, the teacher used to call the students' names who scored high marks in that particular exam. As me and my friends consistently followed the message of the quote,'Stitch in time,saves nine'. We don't face a lot of pressure during exams. But students who procrastinated their studies were used to being too stressed during exams.

Before the exams, whenever I meet any of my friends, they used to tell me that they will score great marks without studying. I was like why their reply should be you know the answers. I just give them one suggestion: you think that I don't have to study, but everyone has the same stress during exams.

The great happiness or sad period used to be after exams when individual subjects' teachers correct their papers and show us in the
class. Some teachers, while showing the paper by saying seat numbers, do a lot of drama. For example:- Once my science teacher said my seat no: 112 please stand up you scored 11 marks in science paper. After hearing this I was shocked but after seeing my paper I used to be happy that the teacher counted after the passing marks. As the passing mark of 20 is 7 and I have scored 19 in that science paper the teacher counted from 8-19 that 19 minus 8 is 11.

Once it was confirmed that we have got good marks we started asking for marks from our other classmates. Kitna Aaya..Kitna Aaya, How much you got?. If someone asks me then I reply,'I Passed'. The feeling of those moments were like flying in the air without a parachute only when you got marks that you expected.

There were a lot of students who compare each other's marks and judge according to it. They don't like to interact with students who scored less marks or get failed in some subjects. I have never judged anyone based on marks. Because I know marks are just a number there is more than this in this materialistic world.

Remember my words:- People as well as you will forget all of your bad marks in the future but you should have that willpower to handle that bad situation when your friends taunt you and compare you based on your marks. Simple, be silent at that moment,everything will be normal.

CHAPTER 19

School Picnic & Field Trip

There is a wonderful quote,'Collect moments, not things' because things can be stolen but thoughts of the moment are never stolen. So I have spended some time with my friends and teachers during school picnics and field trips. We are going to figure it out in this section.

I consider myself to be lucky to be a part of this school as a student. Because there are some schools near where I live, they don't organize class or school picnics. Our school is not from that, we have two class picnics in a year. The first one used to be organized in September and the second one in January or in february.

The definition of picnic & field trip was different for us till class 8th. When our school should go to a resort in September they used to say picnic and when they take us for field trip we think it means we are going to roam places.

I remember in Senior Kg, our school took us to Shangrila resort and then after that I went to a picnic after 5 years in 4th standard . They took us to a great escape resort in Virar and for a field trip in Sanjay Gandhi National Park.

As you all know that in resorts you won't see anything including water and water everywhere. Though we enjoyed it a lot with my friends. I won a mobile there in a game. In the start I lost ten Rs. But after observing and learning from others' mistakes I owned the second time. As the money for playing games was given to my friend, he took that smartphone from me. I was sad, but frequently it got wet in the swimming pool while taking pictures.

In Sanjay Gandhi National Park, we sat in the mini train and had a tour of half of the National Park. We saw deers there. After some time we went deeper inside the Sanjay Gandhi National Park with a mini forest van and saw lions or leopards. I don't recognize them now. Now while sitting and writing this book, while narrating I can feel how I was feeling at that time. It was filled with students and me and some of the friends were standing and was curious and excited to see wild animals.

In 5th standard our school planned to go to the water kingdom this time. As it is a very famous place in Mumbai, the cost was high and my Papa was not ready to send me there. But I convinced him that this is the last picnic and after this I'll not be going anywhere.

We went there by bus, the resort was very huge. There were more than 5 pools, big wave pools, tons of water slides, small rivers, etc. I was there with my friends Samir and Aakash all the time. Because there were less students in our class. There was one slide called as black hole, people told us that it is very scary, don't try that.

Me and my friend Samir Khan attempted to reach the starting point of that slide by walking 200 hundred meters up. Unfortunately Samir's high was below the eligibility to have a ride in black hole slide. But my height was more than the requirement. I was allowed, but Samir was not. I think he was sad and he left me there.

When my chance came for that black hole ride, my heart started beating, legs were not functioning properly. All the people sliding through black hole were shouting and crying. I was thinking about what is special in it. When I tried it, I saw that everything was black in that and I was able to hear some crazy scary, creepy sounds. When I came down, Samir was waiting for me. I told him about what I experienced and then we tried other water slides.

Once they also took us to Rani Baug and Nehru Science Center. In Rani Baug I saw a lot of wild animals like bears, elephants, tiger-like species, crocodiles, huge varieties of indian birds and some species of birds which were brought from foreign countries. In the Nehru Science Center I saw models of some celestial objects. And there was an auditorium where they explained about space and our solar system. The special thing about the auditorium was that it was very dark. We were not able to see anything except the projector images and videos. Some students used to slap anyone and do some drama. I was also part of it.

CHAPTER 20

School Prize Distribution Ceremony

There were a lot of competitions which used to be held in our school for each and every student. For example :- chess,carrom, hand writing competitions, waste out of best, elocution competition, all types of physical games, cricket, kabaddi, fancy dress, etc. All the indoor games and some of the soft competitions used to be held in school while others were on sports day.

The winners of most of the games were awarded with certificates and some with goods in school on 12 January on the occasion of Swami Vivekanand Jayanti in our school hall from the hands of the principal or teachers.

In my school Life I have only got this opportunity to take prizes from our school principal, trustee and teachers only once when I won in a chess competition and in Hindi Easy writing competition. The feeling was inexpressible. When someone calls your name among the hundreds of students, teachers and trustees and when they clap, it gives you the feeling of great ovation and self-respect.But as I had told you that I was not participating in any games during sports day, so I have never won any certificate or medal excluding in chess, kabaddi, cricket and eassy writing competition.

CHAPTER 21

Exam Days

As for getting a job you need to clear an interview identical to it, to become good from others perspective you need to score good marks in your academic exams. Most of the students hate exams and they want to be free from it. But I think exams i.e.tests are the medium through which a shy or introvert guy/student can show his capabilities in studies and can form a positive image, self respect for others.

Let me tell you a real story to understand why exams are good. There was a guy named Manoj. He comes from a village, he had done his schooling from a rural area and was preparing for UPSC civil services examination in Delhi. He had joined a very big coaching named 'Drishti'. It was founded by Ashish Divyakirti Sir. There are 1000's of students in his batch and no one knows him. One day the teacher announced that there will be a test. Hearing this everyone was discussing that if someone scores good marks and his answers are good than Divyakirti sir take his name among the whole crowd and say that this guy has capability to be an IAS officer and once Divyakirti sir says that than really that guy will definitely be that.

Hearing this Manoj studied hard and the day came when Ashish Divyakirti Sir took his and said that Mr.Manoj has capability to be an IAS officer. From that day every single student knew him and respected Manoj. We can learn that even one single moment or thing can make us glow among the crowd. Now it is true, Manoj is a DIG. By the way Manoj was a guy from a village who had failed 12th then drove a rickshaw, worked in a library, worked in a flour mill and then he became successful. If you want to know about the whole journey of DIG Manoj then do read the fictional novel 'Twelfth Fail' by Anurag Tryagi. This book is very inspirational and motivational, this can give you a thrust for working for your goals and achieving it.

If I talk about myself, I was an introverted guy, silent, used to talk very less. I had never tried to ask doubts in class. But still my marks were good and due to that everyone recognized me. When the teacher gives the exam timetable to us we used to be very glad and aim to score full marks in each and every subject. But there is a negative habit of procrastination, the fire, the desire to do great in exams gets cold as the exams neared. I am 100% sure most of the students use youtube for understanding grammar, concepts, etc.

Let's say if we have an English exam tomorrow and we are left out for one day. I used to do a lot of time passing. I used to find some friends in my locality who could play cricket with me. After that I try to find someone who is free and I can talk with him. In such things I was just left out with some time and in those few hours I studied well and used to do great in exams. Now in the present time, i believe that playing unnecessary games during important times is not effective, talking hours with friends is just a waste of time and energy and nothing else.

Instead of doing what mistakes I made, you all learn or do something creative in your free time or when you feel bored in studies or while working. Also I have utilized my free time in writing this book.

CHAPTER 22

Create Win-Win Situation

There is a proverb, "Turn negative situations into positive situations". Whatever we do or not do is a situation either negative or positive. Now let's understand what is the difference between a negative situation and a positive situation.

There were our exams in our school, the paper was a little tough.After giving exams when I came out of the exam hall my lot of friends were saying that the paper was very tough they would hardly score good marks. But my paper was good so I should say,"My paper was good and I can get 40/40". Just think of it, if I say this how they would be feeling. They might be feeling low and this may affect their next paper. Instead of telling reality, I said,"Yes, the paper was very tough but we should forget it and focus on the next paper". Hearing this, they might be thinking that yes everyone's paper was tough and they will be free from stress. So this is how I had always tried to create a win-win situation.

Let's take another example, we all know Himeesh Madan. He is an Entrepreneur, youtuber with 6 million subscribers and public speaker. In one of his programs he called some people on stage and gave each one of them one balloon filled with oxygen gas. He said,"One whose balloon will remain till last, he will receive an award from him". Hearing his words, every balloon holder started bursting others balloons so that he/she could win that game and receive a prize. The result was that one man was able to save his balloon till last and won that game.

Now, how this single winning situation could have turned into a win-win positive situation for everyone. How could I have won? The answer is, if all of them had not burst each other's balloon and remained stopped with their balloon so everyone would have won this game. This also happens in this realistic world. There are some students who don't want to see others going forward then them, employees who don't want to see others going ahead of him/her.

Conclusion is that we can actually make people, friends, and family members feel good by attempting to create a positive win-win situation. This helps people to relate with themselves and bonding between us strengthens.

CHAPTER 23

Marathon in school

In class 3rd during the time of exam, a circular came in the class. It was for students who desire to participate in long run i.e. marathon. The entry fee for it was 50 Rs. All of my classmates filled out the form for participation. I was also willing to participate in that marathon, but at that time I was suffering from a chronic cough disease and was not willing to run such a long race. Also, I was thinking that if I am not able to run in the 100 or 200 meter race properly, how would I complete the race in such a long marathon.

Anyway, I filled the form near Mateshwari garden, Jogeshwari(East). On the day of the event I went to one of my friends' houses who have participated in that same marathon. I went there with his father's bike. I thought there would be only students of our age and standard. But guys I was wrong, there were long and tall personalities waiting for their turn for the marathon. There was a huge crowd gathered there. I got scared and thought of returning back home but I can't leave that place alone. There was my friend and his dad with whom I have gone and with them I have to return home safely and securely.

I met other students from our school, one such friend was Shivam Rai. He was very good and capable of winning that marathon race. After a while they announced the marathon. There were more than 200 participants in my batch. First the members of the organization who organized that marathon ordered us to follow them.After following them for 15-20 minutes They took us to a wide, long open road, I was exhausted from walking for the last 15-20 minutes. I thought about what I would do in the real race. There were cameras, I saw a gun in the hands of someone.

My friend Shivam Rai told me to go stand in the front so that I would get a benefit more than other participants. The referee fired the gun and the race started. I was running very fast and was almost ahead of 95% of the runners, but after running for 500-600 meters I was tired and then my one uncle told me to run slow as I have to run 5 km.As the time passed away I was going backward of others and then in the end I went in the wrong direction unknowingly. I saw no one, so I asked someone and he told me that is the right way. I runned but I was too behind the others, in the way there were only those participants who were too exhausted and walking. I was sweating continuously, I runned with my full capacity and then I found some enthusiastic runners. In the end it started raining and I fell on the ground. I was very sad but after sometime when I reached the destination i.e. the end point I was glad to hear "well done" by the person standing.

I was too tired and exhausted, then suddenly it started raining to its full potential and everyone started getting wet and some of them started dancing on the music system. I rested for half an hour and then I was looking for my bag to have my tiffin, because I was too hungry. I found my bag after a long time and when I was trying to open my tiffin I got a push from some of the people and my tiffin fell on the ground and all the food fell down. I was very annoyed by that person.

After a long while my friend's father came and then he dropped me at my home. I was very tired and my whole body was in pain. After a while I have lunch.

CHAPTER 24

During the time of recess

Rest and break is the only way to relieve pain and refresh our mind. That is the main intention there is little break in the middle segment in the office, school, college, etc. In this time frame all the colleagues in the office of various departments, students from the same class and of different classes are free and get the opportunity to interact with their seniors and juniors. In this chapter I am going to give an overview to you all about what we friends used to do in recess and what freedom we used to get.

Once the recess bell rings I use to go to the washroom and then wash my hands and mouth so that I can feel energetic. After coming back to my place in my class, all the friends asked each other whether what each one of them had brought. I am sharing to you all what I was loving to bring in tiffin, mostly I used to bring maggi and rotti,, potato chapati, fried rice, etc. It is my habit that I always ask others to eat whatever I have brought in tiffin.

We all tried to finish our lunch as fast as we could, because after that we all went outside of the school and sat near the jagdamba mata temple or below the tree at the katta. We all meet all of our friends there and gossip. Still I miss those moments. Sometimes we used to play Kabaddi, hanging on the branches of the banyan tree. Playing pakdam pakdai, having gola, etc. Sharing that long 1 Rs. pepsi with three of the friends.

As the first bell rings we all go back to our classes and then the lectures start. Now we all are energetic and very keen to listen to the teachers and study effectively.

CHAPTER 25

Common thing every student do's in the school

My dear friends, do you remember the first day of your school? Most of you will say.'No'. If you are a high school passed student then do you remember your last day of school ? The answer would be yes for 99% of you. In this portion I am going to trick you and make you think deeper about your past. Read carefully.

Most of us have read till the last minute of our school exams. I mean, reading or learning the answers while going to school by holding our book in two hands until the teacher tells us to close our book and keep it in the bag before the exam starts, still we read while keeping our book in the bag. In my case I don't use to bring books for learning or revising anything before 1 hour of the exam.

Whenever we get any pen or pencil below the benches we used to ask, but mostly no one claims that it's theirs but after some time or few days the real owner of that thing used to claim that it's his/her how we found it?

We all have used pencils sharpened from both sides. We all have heard the story about how we can prepare an eraser by putting sharpened waste from the pencil into the milk for a night. Yes that is fake but still we used to believe in it.

During prayer time sometimes our full focus used to be somewhere else instead of prayer. Over time our habit of saying good morning by rolling our hands was closed. There used to be some students who always passed comments and on that the whole class used to laugh.

When the teacher used to hit us on our palms with the stick we all used to our hands in some bad situations. There used to be some teachers and sirs to whom we were scared most and tried to be active when they were teaching and prayed that they should be absent today.But now we have all the memories which make us travel to the past in our school life.

CHAPTER 26

Friend who left us

It seems like a coincidence happened in my life. One of my best friends, Prince Kanojia from my school, left this materialistic world in class 8th. He joined Swami Vivekanand High School right from Third standard. He was very introvert at that period but over the time when he made some friends like me in class fourth he became more sociable.

When I came in class eighth, Prince Yadav, Kundan Yadav and Prince Kanojia used to sit on an identical bench. We have become very close friends. I have gone to his home as well, whenever I visit his house I used to see half of the area of Jogeshwari East. The skyscrapers, highways, markets, the advertisement banners, vehicles running, etc. In that place there was absolute silence. It was 50-60 meters high. As I have told you all, we used to play cricket on saturday and sunday at various playgrounds together. He was a good bowler in our class.

I have never thought whether one day he will leave us only with the memories of the time that we all have spended with him.Earlier Whenever I was absent in school or I had not completed my notebook I used to take his book for completion. So one day I took his Science 2 book to complete my own book. After that day Prince Knojia was continuously absent for 2-3 days. So I asked my friend Kundan regarding him. He told me,"He is sick".

One night around 11 Pm, I went to an electronics shop to get the new setup box at Pump House,Andheri(East). While returning I met three of my school friends Aadarsh , Samir, Shivam. They were sitting on the bikes parked at the edge of the road and were talking about something. When i went there Shivam Rai tried to pass some message to me but Samir declined to tell him by moving his head. Then I told him to complete what he was trying to say. They all were silent.

So I tried to make the conversation go ahead and said,'Prince Kanojia Bahut Bimar Hai, Bahut Din se school nahi aaya'. They all know whether me and Prince Kanojia are very good friends, and they also know that I didn't know what happened with Prince Kanojia today.

In a very low tone voice they told me that Your Best Friend Prince Kanojia is not alive. Suddenly my heart started beating rapidly and I started sweating.As they were one of the humorous guys. I said,'Don't kid with me, please'. Someone said to me," I know you wont believe this but it's true". Shivam Rai opened his phone to show Prince Kanojia's pic but Samir and Adarsh stopped him from doing that. Then I came back home but we know that the human mind is similar to a monkey. I started thinking about what Samir, Adarsh and Shivam told me.I didn't sleep the whole night.

Next day When I went to school "There was a brief silence in the whole class. Teacher was not present, so I went inside the class and found Kundan sitting on the last bench. I went there and told him that Samir, Adarsh, Shivam were saying that Prince Kanojia is no more. He simply moved his head up and down, which means yes. I head down and upset and immediately started thinking about him. But still I was not believing. The class teacher came and asked me and Kundan what happened with Prince Kanojia. As Kundan was living in his society he said regarding the incident.

But still I was not accepting the reality and then during prayer the announcement was made by the authorities and now it was confirmed and the whole school remained silent and prayed for Prince Kanojia to rest in peace. I didn't write or study anything on that day . After that day whenever I went to school I used to leave one vacant place for Prince Kanojian and wondered if he would come. But after 3-4 weeks I was back to normal. It was very hard to survive in those days without him, only true friends can understand this.

I was having Prince Kanojia's Science 2 book that I had taken for completing my book. Sometimes while removing books from the cupboard I used to read random things written by him in that Science 2 fair book. For example, the chapter notes, the drawing made on the last page, his signature, etc. I used to feel his vibe when I used to see or touch that notebook.

Now whenever I sleep late I usually think about him and wonder what would have happened today if Prince was present. It would be unfair that I write this ebook and don't mention Prince Kanojia's story. 8 months back when I visited that view point near his house from where we can see half of the jogeshwari(East) I felt that I was with him.

CHAPTER 27

Class 10th Story

I came from my village during the rainy season in the month of June-July in Mumbai. School classes were online. As I was late, I haven't joined any coaching classes.I was in search of joining it because school was online and I'll need to have support from a coaching so that I can do well in my boards.

One day I went to meet my tuition teacher Ms.Anita Mam at her house. She asked,"Have you joined any coaching yet?" I replied,"Not yet, I am finding". Then she told me about Amit classes where she was teaching Hindi & geography. She gave me sir's number and told me to visit . Next day my mother and I went to meet Amit Sir. He asked some questions and told me to take demo lectures for a week.

I went in the evening, it was a math lecture that was taken by Amit Sir himself. I found so many of my school friends, for example Shivam, Samir, Adarsh, Kundan, Aayush. I was shocked to see all of them together. I took the lecture and got back home. I thought no classes would be as good as Amit Classes. After a week I was admitted to Amit classes as a regular student.

There was a good study environment. We used to discuss each and every topic with each other. I was consistently doing well. All the teachers were highly qualified. They all were from engineering, Mba, Msc, etc. education background.

CHAPTER 28

My farewell speech day

The end of class 10th was near, there was only 1.5 months left for our board exams. There was our farewell day on 26th february,2022 for class 10th standard students. One day in the morning Our class & English subject teacher told me that Me and Adarsh have to give a speech on the farewell day. At that moment I told her yes. But after some days I started overthinking and giving negative suggestions to myself about how you can speak among such a large audience.What if you get stuck in the middle during your speech? What do people think about you? What will your teachers think about you?,etc.

I used to count how many days I have left for my farewell day. 44,43,42.....12 still I was procrastinating and forwarding my speech preparation the next day and now I was left out with hardly 7-8 days. One day I sat and dreamed that if I succeed in delivering an astounding speech among the students and my respected teachers, yes it will be memorable for all of us throughout their life. I prepared speech, I didn't write the whole speech, instead I just wrote the points I want to talk about.For example, Saying good morning to everyone, contribution of other staff members such as peon, watchmen, swipers and of teachers, what school really taught me?What I learnt from respective teachers? How do I feel in school? Some memories of the past ? Some left out teachers? I read a book titled 'Obstacle is the way' which really taught me that if you wanna succeed and master any skill then you'll have to take risks and see it as an opportunity.

As I was left out with just 7-8 days I started repeating those points in my mind for the rest of the days which were in my hand. Now that day has come and we have to wear formal dress and come to school for that function. I was too nervous and sad. Nervous because I have to deliver a speech that I have never done and sad because this was the last day of our school life . I woke up at 7 Am and just went through the highlighted points I have written on that gray-white paper. Believe me guys I have written very wide and deep points and ideas on that paper, I know that if I am successful in elaborating the whole points and delivering the speech then everyone can become emotional and remember this moment throughout their life.

Before this day I have never addressed such a huge crowd and delivered a speech. While coming to school I met so many of my friends we shaked hands and moved on. While entering the school I said,'Good Morning Sir" to our school watchmen. He was happy from the outside but may be unhappy from inside. He replied same to you. Then I entered my school and saw many students in black and white coats, girls in angel dresses. Some of them looked towards me. I shaked hands with them and entered my class. I said good morning to my class teacher and then I took some pictures with her and some of my friends.

At 8:45 everyone went into the school hall for the beginning of this memorable moment. I sat in the right corner bench with some of my friends, for example Rishu, Adarsh, Arpit. The staff members from our school arranged the mic and speaker. The anchoring was done by Kavita Miss and some class 9th students. First thing first our school Principal Manoj Sir addressed the crowd and then names for delivering speeches by students were started. I was very scared, nervous, feared, my heart was beating, I was sweating, etc. I asked one of my friends, Adarsh, how he would do on stage? He was very confident. He replied,'Everything will be okay'.

As there was no language barrier, you may give the speech in English or hindi. Some of them were delivered in hindi and some in english. All of them had brought written material so they used to read from it and say. Anyway, they all delivered the speech very well . The whole crowd used to clap when they finished their speech. After this Adarsh's name was called out and he also did a great job. Now I saw that everyone has done very well, they don't even stop or get stuck while reading. I was wondering whether I would also bring written material to deliver a speech. But the situation was not in my hands. I was also having stammering and suturing problems. This is an incurable disease and you can cure it by practicing public speaking. Thanks to yoga and meditation which helped me to cure it 90%.

Now it's my turn, the speaker announced my name 'Prince Yadav' . Please come on stage to share your feelings and wonderful thoughts. I wiped my face with the handkerchief and went with confidence. I said to myself that I can do this. There were approximately 180+ students , more than 25+teachers, principal trustees, members of authority, staff members,etc. I thought that all people have done a lot for me and other students and I have to just speak a few lines on it. With this motive I started speaking without bothering about anything. I spoked without any script and all the thoughts, ideas & feelings were coming from my heart. I completed my speech and at the end everyone clapped with joy. Our Marathi teacher Latika miss smiled and told me that I have done a great job.

When I sat on the bench Everyone was staring at me and they were very glad to hear all the things I have said during my speech. Dubey sir said,'Well done Yadavji'. After this our school principal, teachers, trustee and other members presented their speech. Now I was totally free from all the fears with whom I was living from the last 1.5 months.
I got the confidence that yes, you have the power to speak on stage. Later, when I met my class teacher, she was satisfied and exhilarated with what points I have covered and presented there.

I was shy and underconfident, sometimes I used to stammer as well, but still I was able to do my job on the farewell day. That was a remarkable moment for me. Now at this time I think I have improved a lot when we talk about communication.

CHAPTER 29

Mistakes I made in my school Life

There is a saying in English,"If you're not making mistakes then you are not a human being". After being a class 11 student I believe that there are a lot of mistakes that I have made in school. I wish someone would have guided me and told me to avoid such mistakes then I would have been better than what I am today in this present situation. Read this chapter carefully, because this is very one of the most important chapters of this book.

If you are in school and reading this book then you have a chance to know about the mistakes and implement what is said. But if you are from a higher class or above this, still you should read this chapter so that you can really guide the smaller ones or if you are making this mistakes now also so you can make sure to avoid it.

1. Fear of asking questions in class

I am pretty sure 99% of readers have never tried to ask doubts or quotations in school life. Simply, they used to move their heads up and down when the teacher asked,"Any doubt?". Student replies,"No". This is actually not helpful in long term games. Most of us shy in asking questions or doubt, most of us are scared to ask, most of them think that they have the internet, mobile phones and they will clear their doubts by using it why they should ask and waste our and teachers time but in the end they struggle. It's better to stand and ask doubts immediately.

2.Not socializing with people

Everyone was a stranger for each one of us until we didn't communicate with others and spent some time with them. Have you ever seen some students in your school, college or people in your office? If they are present or not you won't be able to feel their vibe. In my school life I had that kind of personality. Yes, being silent has too many benefits but still we should at least speak something that shows our presence.

I wish I would have been more sociable in school so that teachers and students would have recognised me well. So you all can learn from this small mistake.

3.Fear of failing

Atychiphobia is an intense fear of failure. It comes from the Greek word "atyches," meaning "unfortunate."People with atychiphobia may avoid any situation where they see a potential for failure, such as an exam or job interview. It can also mean being afraid of a failed relationship, a failed career or being a disappointment to others.

The fear often becomes self-fulfilling. For example, if you're so scared of failing a test that you refuse to take the test, you may end up failing an entire class.Fear of failure can lead to a broad range of emotional and psychological problems, including shame, depression, anxiety, panic attacks or low self-esteem. It may negatively affect how you perform at school or work, or how you interact with friends and family members.

I don't think that it was my negative thought of failing. Even this thing has helped me to imagine what will happen if I choose certain paths whenever it comes to a decision.

4. Not participated in sports events

Right from class 6th I have never participated in sports events organized by our school. I was believing that how well I perform, execute I am going to lose. So I used to sit at home and study for exams. But now after passing out from high school I wonder why I didn't participate in such events? I believe that I would have gained lots of experience from it.

5.Procrastination

Procrastination is the act of putting off doing something that you should do till another day or time, because you do not want to do it. It is a common problem which you will find in 99% of the world's population. Every student is the prey of this effect which leads to stress, pressure, anxiety in the termination phase of exams, project submission, etc.

We cannot conclude that procrastination is not good every time. We have the world famous 'Monalisa' painting designed by Leonardo Da Vinci. It took 16 years to paint. This painting's total value is $1billion. This book is also the result of procrastination. In the end I got too many chapter ideas which I have included in this book.

CHAPTER 30

What School Taught Me

I'm probably sure you all know the proverb 'School is temple and teacher is God'. Yes, this is absolutely true and we are disciples there. When I was in school I never thought that I am out of my house meant I was feeling the same vibe as in my home. The teachers were caring for each and everyone, he/she knew the strength and weakness of each and everyone and so they used to guide according to it.

I have also told this in my farewell speech that I have learned moral values, life lessons from each and every teacher. School was a platform where all of us were united, there was no boundness of caste, creed, religion. Also it was the only place where we gathered together. School plays an important role in building the foundation for our upcoming life. It is a platform for getting to interact with people from different backgrounds, and share each other's knowledge, experience, etc. with each other. I learned to treat others very well.

School creates a lot of opportunities for many energetic and enthusiastic students in the form of sports events, various indoor competitions and freedom to show our creativity and talent. Also it taught me how to face small-small challenges. As we want to go school we used to wake up early in the morning.

CHAPTER 31

My message to all the readers

Hi readers, I hope you all have read each and every chapter and enjoyed reading this book. I am sure you have filled the inner child in you. While reading you would have missed some of your school friends, teachers and others. Also you have got to know more about me and my inner personality during school life.

If you really love it, don't forget to take a picture of this book and post your experience on facebook, instagram, twitter, linkedin, snapchat, etc. wherever you are active. Share the experience and stories of this book with your friends, family. This book can be a special gift for small childrens, elders, older. Do give them. Also give your feedback and rating to this book on amazon. Due to this we can make this book more reachable to other readers.

Share your experience, feedback, your honest opinion with me on instagram, Linkedin, I'll be glad to see that.

Note

www.ingramcontent.com/pod-product-compliance
Lightning Source LLC
LaVergne TN
LVHW021141160826
845679LV00023B/2003

* 9 7 9 8 8 8 9 2 3 7 5 9 4 *